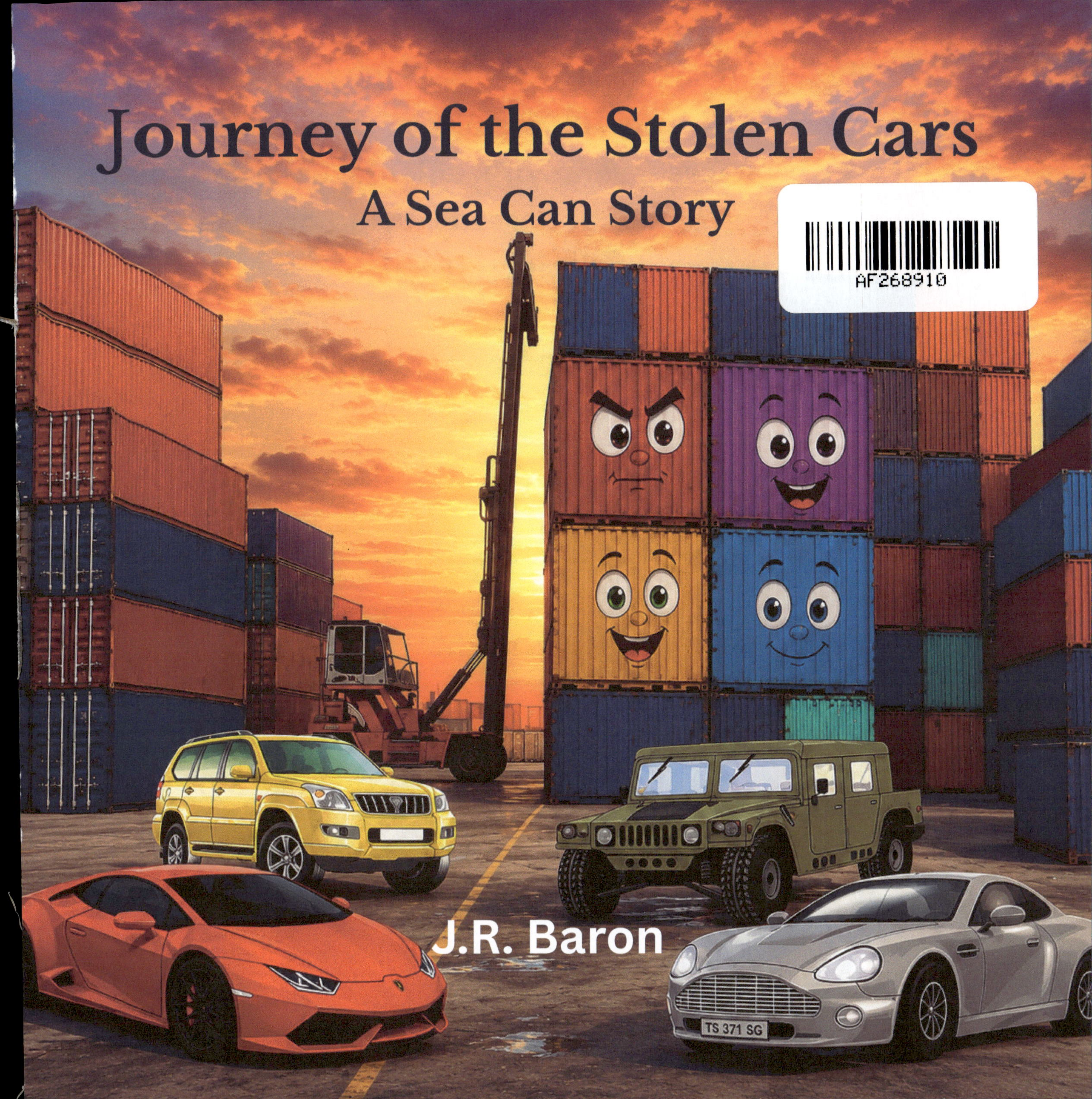

Journey of the Stolen Cars
A Sea Can Story
J.R. Baron
AF268910
TS 371 SG

Titles in The Sea Can Series

All Aboard

Lost At Sea

Journey of the Stolen Cars
ISBN: 978-1-7380722-3-1

For more information, go to www.seacanstories.ca

For my big kids -
Linnea and Liam.

The sun set over a quiet evening in the shipping container storage yard.

Suddenly, the vroom-vroom of speeding engines sounded closer by the second.

"What's that noise?" whispered Kay to her three sea can friends, Vim, Chase and Floyd.

"Cars!" Vim exclaimed. She loved anything fast with a high rev engine.

"Whoa," Chase marveled. "Nice ones!"

"I have a bad feeling about this," said Floyd.

Four luxury vehicles pulled up close to the sea cans.

Their drivers got out quickly.

"That was just too easy," said the first one. He looked young and nervous.

"I know," said the second young man. "All I had to do was bounce a signal off the electronic key in the house. You told me it was going to be easy, but I didn't think it was going to be that easy!" He laughed nervously.

"How can people be so careless?" mocked a third young voice. "They could use steering wheel locks, key fob boxes or even a security camera! It took me less than five minutes to clone this blank key fob!" he bragged.

"Don't get too confident," said an older man with a deep gravelly voice. "We have to give these hot cars some cool down time here. Then we'll get them on the next ship to cross the Atlantic."

Vim recognized the voice.
 "Hey, I know that guy! Mic! He works here. I often here him telling stories in the rail yard," Vim said.

"And I think that's just where we're going," concluded Floyd.

Mic, the man with the gravelly voice, opened up the sea cans. He put down a ramp and each man drove a stolen vehicle inside one of four sea cans. They slammed their rear doors shut and locked them tight.

    "I've got a four-wheel drive all-terrain military type vehicle!" screamed Vim. She was so excited.

 "Mine's a luxury brand!" Chase shouted nervously. "This cannot be right."

He knew the car's rightful owners would be so upset.

"And there are baby car seats in it!" Chase cried.

"This red sport car is lovely," said Kay, "but there are leftover takeout boxes in it. I'm going to stink". She hated being messy and out of control.

"While I can appreciate the impressiveness of this brand new off-road vehicle," said Floyd, "I'm afraid it's stolen. We're going to have to figure out a way to alert the police".

"We're on the move!" shouted Vim.

"This is all happening too quickly!" screamed Chase.

"Stay calm and try not to panic," Floyd said in a voice that sounded steadier than he felt.

The four sea cans sat in silence on their chassis, as the truck drivers sped through the night. They needed to get the shipping containers to the rail yard where they could cool down.

"Shh!" commanded Kay. "I hear a beeping noise".

"It's the GPS tracker in your sport's car!" Floyd yelled. "It's alerting the owner of the vehicle's location!"

"I hear one in mine too!" Chase yelled.

"That must be what Mic meant by cooling off," Vim said.

"Right!" Floyd agreed. "Once the tracker battery dies, they'll be harder to find!"

"We've got to do something before that happens!" screamed Chase.

BEEP!
BEEP!
BEEP!
BEEP!

"It's true," Floyd agreed. "If we wind up on a ship crossing the Atlantic and end up on another continent, it's going to be very hard to return these stolen cars back to their rightful owners".

"I can't believe this is happening to us," marveled Kay. "But I have to admit, the speed and organization of this illegal operation is blowing my mind!"

"We're slowing down," Vim said. She could feel the rigs pulling off the highway.

RAIL
YA

"We're at the railyard." Floyd said.

The drivers quickly unloaded the sea cans off of the truck chassis and stacked them on top of each other.

"Good job, boys," Mic said. "I'll be back here in the morning to load them onto the train. Then I've got someone at the other end to get them on the freighter ship. You will get three times the money for these vehicles overseas than what you could get for them here!"

The three young men laughed nervously. Then they got into their trucks and drove away, leaving the sea cans in the dark and empty rail yard.

"I've got an idea!" said Kay. "After we fell off the freighter ships into the ocean, companies ensured that we had our own GPS trackers installed. If we set all of ours off at once, it will alert our owners and they will notice we are missing."

"Yes!" screamed Chase. "And they'll come looking for us!"

"Let's hope so," said Floyd.

The next morning, Mic arrived early. He hopped onto a forklift to begin moving the sea cans towards the train tracks.

Suddenly, blaring sirens burst into the rail yard. Police cars surrounded the four sea cans.

"Open the doors," yelled an officer.

Mic looked like he was going to run, but he was surrounded.

Slowly he unlocked Kay, Vim, Chase and Floyd to reveal the stolen cars inside.

Another officer let out a long whistle. "You are under arrest," he said as he cuffed Mic. "We are seizing these cars immediately and we'll make sure they get back to their rightful owners!"

POLICE

The next day, Kay, Vim, Chase and Floyd were resting comfortably on rail cars wells. They were headed back to their storage yard.

"For once it feels good to be empty," laughed Vim.

The train whistle gave two long blasts and lurched forward.

"Ready?" asked Kay.
"Set!" exclaimed Vim.
"Go!" shouted Chase.
"All Aboard," sighed Floyd.

125-T

Stolen Cars Facts

- In 2022 alone, millions of dollars worth of luxury cars were stolen in Canada, put into shipping containers and sailed across the Atlantic Ocean to be resold illegally in other countries.
- For more information, go to: www.cbc.ca/news and search auto theft Canada.
- Trackers and tracking apps help people to locate important and expensive items, like luxury cars.
- Car owners can use a variety of methods to slow down and prevent car thefts, such as steering wheel locks, key fob protectors, and security cameras.

- If you suspect a car has been stolen, call the police.
- Investigative teams work together to prevent car thefts and recover stolen cars.
- On February 8th, 2024, the Canadian government held its first National Summit on Combatting Auto Theft. For more information, go online at Public Safety Canada: National Summit on Combatting Auto Theft.

<u>About the Author</u>
When she's not teaching, J.R. Baron can be found close to rivers, lakes and oceans.
Her primary students inspired The Sea Can Stories when they became curious about shipping containers. At that time, J.R. Baron could not find any children's stories about shipping containers, so she wrote her own. For more information go to www.seacanstories.ca

The Journey of the Stolen Cars
ISBN: 978-1-7380722-3-1
Ecoinquiry Publishing